The Reason Why We Sing

Introducing Black Pentecostal Spirituality

Clifton Clarke

Minister in the New Testament Church of God
Part-time Tutor on the Intercultural Theology Programme,
Nottingham University

GROVE BOOKS LIMITED
RIDLEY HALL RD CAMBRIDGE CB3 9HU

Contents

1. Introduction 3

2. The Roots of Black Holiness—Pentecostalism 4

3. The Theological Content of Black Pentecostal Spirituality 10

4. Black Pentecostal Spirituality and Black Culture 20

5. Conclusion 24

Acknowledgements

I would like to acknowledge Marcia, my wife, for her support and encouragement. I would also like to thank David Jones, Vicar of All Souls, Radford, for the times we have spent theologically reflecting on street corners and in the church car park, Scott Ellington, for his honesty and insight, and Valerie Howe, Pitman Brown and Peter Stapleton for their thoughts and reflections.

The Cover Illustration is by Peter Ashton

First Impression May 1997
ISSN 0262-799X
ISBN 1 85174 343 X

1
Introduction

In recent years much has been written concerning the black pentecostal tradition in Britain. It has become the subject matter for a multiplicity of essays, articles and dissertations. However, many of these works have focused on the black pentecostal tradition in Britain from a sociological perspective, concentrating their attention on such matters as its rapid growth in the early years, its style of worship, its doctrine, and its ethical codes. In the main, they have not yet captured the multi-faceted and rather complex spirituality which animates its beliefs and practices.

This may be because black pentecostal spirituality belongs to a largely oral culture, which means it is not easily accessible. This is compounded by the fact that much of the work on this issue has been written by white Europeans looking in on this tradition,[1] usually with an academic interest, which means that their encounter with our tradition is restricted by time. It is only in these last few years that some black pentecostals have produced printed documents capturing something of the social and political dynamism of Pentecost.[2] Whilst it is very easy and perhaps convenient to subscribe to a simplistic and stereotypical understanding of black pentecostal spirituality—not looking beyond the novelty of the gospel singing—any serious investigation will reveal a complex, eclectic spirituality spanning centuries and continents of the world.

In this booklet it is my intention to explore the depth and trace the journey of this spirituality. By doing this I hope to stimulate potential partnership and dialogue between black pentecostal spirituality and Protestant and Catholic spirituality. My own experience of black pentecostalism comes from twenty years as a member of a church within the black pentecostal tradition, as well as five years as a minister in the New Testament Church of God.

Terminology is important for this issue. You will have noticed by now that I have used the term 'black pentecostal tradition' instead of terms like 'black church' or 'West Indian church.' That is because these other descriptions do not fit the church that I am a member of and are not helpful terms from a pastoral perspective. Although the church I serve in has a predominantly black membership, it remains a church for the 'who so ever will.' The very idea of 'church,' the *ecclesia*, carries with it the idea of a multiracial commonality cutting across culture and gender for Jew and Gentile, male and female, bond and free (Gal 3.28). This for me contradicts the notion of a 'black church'—or a 'white church' for that matter. It is also contrary to the spirit of Pentecost, which was characterized by the breaking down of racial barriers both at Jerusalem in Acts 2 and in 1906 during the Azusa Street revival. The term 'black-led church' is also a misnomer because most

1   See W Hollenweger, *Pentecostal Between Black and White* (Christian Journals Ltd, 1974) p 20.
2   *ibid.*

of the prominent churches within the pentecostal tradition in Britain have extensive white leadership, usually based in the United States. I use the term 'black' to refer to people of African decent. A detailed discussion on terminology may be found in the first chapter of Joel Edwards' *Let's Praise Him Again.*[3] I use the term 'spirituality' to mean the whole person in relation to God and rest of the community—the total person in a total context.

In this booklet, I will explore the historical background to black pentecostal spirituality, drawing out the major influences that have contributed to the black pentecostal tradition as it appears today in Britain. I have a particular interest in drawing out the influence that African traditional religion has had upon it. I will then look at the theological content of this brand of pentecostalism and its significance as it appears in many of the black pentecostal churches in Britain. Throughout this booklet I hope to demonstrate the importance of living and worshipping in a cultural community setting, whilst facing the tensions and contradictions that this often presents. This booklet is intended to illustrate what black pentecostal spirituality can contribute to the other rich Christian traditions that exist within the church as a whole.

2

The Roots of Black Holiness—Pentecostalism

Black pentecostal spirituality is an eclectic spirituality drawing on a wide range of influences, traditions and cultures. It is a spirituality which is not cerebral and intellectual, conforming to western logic and discursiveness, but one which comes alive in song, in dance and in folklore.[4] It is a spirituality shaped by the journey across the middle passage from Africa to the black Diaspora. A spirituality rooted in the lived experience of this journey, often filled with contradictions of suffering and pain, of tears and of laughter, of joy and sadness, of life and yet of death.

The Pentecostal Revival
Most church historians maintain that the pentecostal movement in its modern form dates back to the beginning of the twentieth century in the United States. However, it is important to pentecostals that this is not seen as the beginning of the movement *per se*, but as the continuing fulfilment of the prophesy in Joel 2, often called the 'latter rain' downpouring. The first Pentecost, they maintain, took

---

3 Joel Edwards (ed), *Let's Praise Him Again: An Africa-Caribbean Perspective on Worship* (Kingsway, 1992).
4 Sehon Goodridge, 'Liberating Spirituality' in Simon of Cyrene Theological Journal, 1994, p 5.

4

place in Jerusalem somewhere around AD 34, in which the same Spirit that was present in the life of Jesus descended and empowered his followers and created a new community. Pentecostals hold that the same 'fire from heaven' that filled the upper room with tongues of fire heralding in a new era in Christian history was experienced once again in an explosive manner, with great consequences and power, during the 1906 Azusa Street revival in Los Angeles, USA. After the original fire from heaven, something went wrong. Instead of announcing the glad news to all the nations, Christians became smug and indolent. They lapsed into writing meticulous creeds and inventing lifeless rituals.[5] Although there were sprinklings of blessings here and there, on the whole the church was inert. The pentecostal revival is the church reawakening to the power of the Holy Spirit which was evident by the speaking with tongues. It is this renaissance that is seen as the beginning of the pentecostal movement.

The theological basis of the pentecostal movement has been traced back to Charles F Parham's Bethel Bible school in 1906 at Topeka, Kansas. Parham and his students established a theological connection between speaking in tongues and the 'baptism in the Holy Spirit' which has stayed with pentecostalism ever since.[6] Although Parham is credited with establishing the theological basis upon which pentecostal revival was built, it was William Joseph Seymour, a black 'Holiness' preacher born in 1870, who was the main personality and pioneer behind this movement.[7] Seymour was born to former slaves Simon and Phillis Seymour and raised up as a Baptist with strong 'Holiness' leanings. In 1906 Seymour enrolled as a student of the Bethel Bible School, which was in the Holiness tradition. Parham, however, a Ku Klux Klan sympathizer, did not think it was a good idea, though he permitted him to listen to lectures seated on a chair outside an opened window. On a rainy day he was allowed to sit in the hallway where he could hear the lectures with the door left ajar. Seymour had become convinced of the truth of Parham's teaching on the Holy Spirit baptism, so much so that it drove him to Los Angeles, California to preach the new teaching. On 14th April 1906, Seymour held his first service at 312 Azusa Street, in an old run-down warehouse. A month after the beginning of the mission, more than a thousand people were trying to enter the old stable to witness this strange phenomenon of people speaking in tongues. The services were electric and people flocked to the altar to receive the baptism of the Holy Spirit. During the revival, barriers came down between black and white and Hispanics, clergy and laity, male and female, because the baptism in the Holy Spirit was available to all who believed. It was the teaching and preaching of William Seymour that led to what is today known as the great pentecostal revival which not long after could be found in Canada, England, Scandinavia, Germany, China, India, Africa and South America.

5   Harvey Cox, *Fire from Heaven*, p 47.
6   It is perhaps worth making clear here that pentecostalism sees the 'baptism in the Holy Spirit' as a second experience, separate from conversion and subsequent to it. It is possible to be a Christian and have not yet received this 'baptism in the Holy Spirit.'
7   Leonard Lovett, *Dictionary of Pentecostal and Charismatic Movements* (Regency, 1988) p 780.

African Traditional Religion

One must not underestimate the lasting influence that African traditional religion has on black pentecostal spirituality. For many people the idea of an 'African traditional religion' is new. Western anthropologists such as Edward Tylor and Evans Pritchard argued that African religions were nothing more than the savage animist religions of primitive people.[8] African theologians and teachers of African religious studies are divided between those who see a single system of belief having a diversity of manifestations in the different cultures and customs within Africa, and those who argue that Africa has a plurality of religions.[9] Despite this, there is now general agreement that African traditional religion is a more-or-less coherent belief system with its own internal logic.

It was from this base that the black slaves encountered Christian theology and spirituality from a western perspective. African traditional religion was the faith of the black slaves, the strongest element in their background and probably the greatest influence upon their thinking and living. Their understanding of Western Christianity must be seen against this background, and this explains why aspects of Western Christianity are much more readily understood and adopted by Christians of African decent. Important elements include the following.

a) Belief in a Supreme God

According to African philosophy, God is the origin and sustenance of all things. The notion of a supreme God is the most minimal and fundamental idea of God found in all African societies.[10] God is not a philosophical proposition or an anaemic thought but a life-giving spirit both immanent and transcendent.[11] He is the God of a million galaxies yet the God who is closer than my own soul. God is life, resurrecting, reviving and quickening all that is lifeless. God is power—healing, transforming, saving and destroying. This is how Mbiti describes the African concept of God:

'God is outside and beyond his creation, so that it is not outside of him or of his reach. God is simultaneously transcendent and immanent.'[12]

This idea of the immanence and the transcendence of God is very important for the African concept of God and is often misunderstood by white Europeans, many of whom still hold to the colonial definition of the African God, which is of an African King in a sleep of idleness, too great to interest himself in the affairs of the world. Sadly this notion of God is still associated with the theology of black pentecostals, who, it is often said, are more concerned with the God in heaven

---

8   E Tylor, *Primitive Culture* (London: H Holt & Co, 1871); E Prichard, *Witchcraft, Oracles, and Magic Among the Azande* (Oxford: The Clarendon Press, 1937).
9   See the works of J Mbiti, *African Religions and Philosophy* (London: SPCK, 1969) and E Idowu, *African Traditional Religion* (London: SPCK, 1973).
10   John Mbiti, *Concepts of God in Africa* (London: SPCK, 1970).
11   R Gerloff, *A Plea for British Black Theology* (Peter Lang, 1992) p 61.
12   Mbiti, *op cit.*

than the God walking the earth. However, a close examination of African theology of God, as with the churches in the black pentecostal tradition, will reveal that this simply is not the case. I will return to this issue latter on in the booklet.

b) Oral Culture

When I use the term 'oral culture' I refer to a preference for unwritten means of communicating and storing information; it does not mean 'illiterate' or 'non-literary.' Traditional African culture is orally based. It is forever changing, growing, developing; it is alive. It is not fixed or written down, but expressed through dreams, visions, testimonies, songs, dance, sharing and fellowship. There is, no doubt, a curious ambiguity in the African and Caribbean personality in that we are usually reluctant to commit to print what we can express better orally. This oral culture, however, has affected our approach to theology, which cannot be located in the volumes of systematic theological—much to the frustration of academic researches—but in the lives of the people in relation to each other.

c) Spirits

Spirits in African culture are ubiquitous. There is no area of the earth, no object or creature, which has not a spirit of its own or which cannot be inhabited by a spirit. There are therefore spirits of trees (that is spirits that inhabit trees) rocks, mountains and hills, forest and bush, rivers and watercourse. Some spirits are even considered to have been created as a 'race' by themselves. According to Mbiti, most people seem to believe that spirits are what remains of human beings when they die physically: 'spirits are the destiny of man and beyond them God.'

For the African, spirits are a part of everyday life; they know nothing of the sacred/secular divide of Western thought. This traditional understanding of spirits is one of the reason why black people naturally gravitate towards pentecostalism and explains a rapid and escalating black following in a relatively short amount of time.

The notion of being overcome or immersed in the Spirit was nothing new to the Africans and was all too similar to the experience of spirit possession.[13] It was the influence of the African slaves during the early pentecostal camp meetings that introduced the ecstatic behaviour—which Parham called 'crude Negroism of Southland'—during which the Holy Spirit came upon a person. This was characterized by jerking, shouting, dancing, rolling on the floor, and all that now is associated with 'being in the Spirit.' Evil spirits are also very commonplace in African culture which again has a prominent role in black pentecostalism.

d) Worship

The style of worship of the black pentecostal tradition is perhaps one of the clearest evidences of the African link. For the African, worship involves the whole being—to worship is to give yourself totally to God, body, soul and spirit. It is to

---

13 John Mbiti, *African Religion and Philosophy* (SPCK, 1969).

become so overwhelmed and endowed by the Spirit that you become one with the Supreme and Almighty. It is from this ancient tradition that black music has developed into what it is today.

e) Agents of Healing

To be struck with a fatal illness in an African context is no accident, but the direct result of an evil spirit or a bad omen. To combat the illness, a combination of the scientific and the supernatural is needed. The African priest is therefore a holy man and a doctor of medicine. This notion of the harmony between the supernatural and natural, the physical and the spiritual, is central to African philosophy, and this has contributed to the important place of the minister as an agent of healing in the black pentecostal tradition. It is right at the centre of black pentecostal spirituality.

Black Slave Religion in America and the Caribbean

The pentecostal movement was born amidst the fleeting shadows of slavery in America. This was the same milieu in which the negro spirituals emerged. It was the black experience of slavery that created their unique sound and rhythm. The spirituals enabled the blacks to preserve their African identity whilst living at the mercy of white slave owners, combining African music—which served not so much as entertainment but as oral history—with the Christian message. Traditionally, African music functioned as recorded history, the story of the life of the community: initiation, birth, death, marriage, belief. The spirituals, then, are historical songs that speak of the pain and suffering of black people; they tell the story of a people striving for humanity and dignity in a society of oppression and racial hatred. Unlike the blues, their secular counterpart, the spirituals usually had a glimmer of hope beneath the note of despair that 'trouble won't last always.' A good example of this is the song:

Nobody knows the trouble I've seen,
Nobody knows my sorrows,
Nobody knows the trouble I've seen,
Glory Hallelujah.

Although one can sense the despair in the lyrics of this song, emphasised by the mood of the tune, the 'glory hallelujah' is a high note of praise, indicative of the inherent contradiction or ambivalence of the spiritual. One of the fascinations of the spiritual is the ability of the black slaves to hold together hope and despair, joy and sorrows, death and life in their music.[14]

The spirituals were by no means a reflection of the black slave's striving toward social and political liberation, nor were they the result of an escapist attitude resigned to slavery whilst here on earth. On the contrary, as John Lovell has

---

14 James Cone, *The Spirituals and the Blues* (Orbis, 1992) p 19.

shown, the spiritual was a reflection of the social life of slaves which was based on their African background.[15] The songs, then, were used to counteract the dehumanization that they confronted on a daily basis.

The Holiness Movement

The ethical roots of black pentecostalism go back to the 'Holiness' movement of the mid-nineteenth century in the United States. This movement was born out of the concern that Methodism was failing to live up to the Wesleyan tradition of sanctification and the centrality of the Bible. At a time when traditional Christianity was being undermined by modern theology and clerical formalism, it sought to regain ground through a re-emphasis on biblical holiness and the necessity of sanctification. Believers were called to strive for Christian perfection through the process of sanctification. Sanctification was exemplified by separation from the things which were associated with 'worldliness,' such as drinking alcohol, smoking, gambling, swearing, wearing of lavish jewellery, and social dancing. This 'Holiness code' is still alive and well in most black pentecostal churches today.

The Holiness movement taught that sanctification followed conversion. Sanctification here was understood in the Wesleyan tradition as distinct in time and content from conversion and was also called the second blessing or associated with a 'baptism of the Spirit.' This is known as the 'two-stage way of salvation.' The pentecostal revival actually made the 'baptism of the Holy Spirit' a third stage; for them this was distinct from sanctification. This was the doctrine commonly accepted by the pentecostal movement until about 1908, when it was challenged by W H Durham, a respected evangelist who argued that conversion and sanctification were simultaneous and that sanctification was a continuous process throughout life—'progressive sanctification.'[16] Pentecostal churches still differ on this doctrinal issue.

15 John Lovell, 'The Social Implication of the Negro Spiritual' in Bernard Katz (ed), *The Social Implication of Early Negro Music in the United States* (Arno Press, 1969) p 25. On this see further James Cone *op cit.*
16 Water Hollenweger, *The Pentecostals* (SCM, 1972).

3
The Theological Content
of Black Pentecostal Spirituality

In this chapter I will be looking at some of the ordinances, sacraments and distinctive practices within black pentecostal spirituality. My aim here is to provide theological reflection which will hopefully lead to a deeper understanding of our spirituality. This section may be particularly useful for ecumenical dialogue and multicultural worship. The spirituality that I will be presenting here will be reflective to a greater and lesser degree of churches within the black pentecostal tradition in general. However, it will be more reflective of the black pentecostal churches within the Trinitarian tradition, especially from within my own denomination, the New Testament Church of God.

The Holy Spirit
The Holy Spirit is a good place to start this exploration. It is here where it all began, 'Pentecost.' And it is of central importance in understanding black pentecostal spirituality because of the influence of African traditional views of the spirit-world.

Very soon after I became a Christian, in the New Testament Church of God (NTCOG), it was clear to me that I was not actually *bona fide* until I received the 'baptism of the Holy Spirit.'[17] Although it was most certainly not a condition for faith, it was certainly the rite of passage that distinguished those Christians who were less spiritually experienced from those who were more experienced. It did not matter how theologically astute or versed in Scripture you were, or how well you could construct and deliver a sermon; if you had not received the 'baptism of the Holy Spirit' you had not yet started, much less arrived. Ideally one's baptism in the Spirit should be at a church service, so that the elders of the church can hear the person being baptized speak with tongues, which is believed to be the authenticating mark of the experience. If you were not fortunate enough to receive it in a public place, such as a service, then during prayer elders will listen to hear you speak in tongues and confirm whether or not what you have is the real thing.

This 'baptism of the Holy Spirit' serves several important functions in the context of a black-led pentecostal church. It allows the whole church community to participate and bear witness that God has reinforced your conversion by baptizing you with his Spirit. It is divine confirmation—similar to the dove resting on the head of Jesus during his baptism by John the Baptist—that God has saved and

---

17 For an analysis of the New Testament's use of the term 'baptism in the Holy Spirit' see David Newman *What We are About to Receive: the Holy Spirit in initiation and experience* (Grove Pastoral booklet P 7).

empowered you for service. I remember the day after I received the 'baptism of the Holy Spirit'—which incidentally was the most powerful spiritual experience I have ever had—feeling a strong sense of relief and joy. Part of my joy was due to the fact that I was now initiated. I had moved from being numbered among the 'unfilled' and having to labour at the altar for the infilling of the Holy Spirit, to being among the spiritual élite, those who were called to pray for those who were not yet spiritually initiated. The idea behind this emphasis is the belief that becoming a Christian is much more than an intellectual acceptance of a rational faith, but rather an experience of the transcendent God or, in the words of Rudolf Otto the encounter with '*mysterium tremendum et fascinans*.'[18]

The 'baptism of the Spirit' then, not only provides evidence of direct contact with God, but it also reinforces the spiritual solidarity of the church community. Added to this, it further allows the individuals to officiate in a leadership capacity within church. It is also essential for anyone who feels called to the lay or ordained ministry.

It might be suggested that the role of the 'baptism of the Holy Spirit' is similar to the role played by the spirit possession trance in African traditional religion. This experience in an African context demonstrates to those who are observing that the dancer—who normally is a spiritual healer—is being possessed by a supernatural spirit, thus giving him special powers. Extrinsically, this possession trance is sometimes enacted in the services of black pentecostal churches during which a person or persons will shake, jerk, walk, or run up and down the aisles speaking in tongues and prophesying.

This behaviour is sometimes exaggerated, particularly by the less educated members who may have little influence within the life of the church. Under normal circumstances they may not feel confident to articulate their frustration or demonstrate their concerns. This lack of social and ecclesiastical status is sometimes compensated for under the possession trance. By being the object of divine medium, in which the member is transfixed, speaking with a robotic tone of voice and observed by the entire congregation, the member who had very little power is now the agent of supernatural power. Most churches are now addressing the issue of the edifying role of the Holy Spirit in the life of the church, conforming to the apostle Paul's teaching on this matter. However, there are times when emotionalism and personalities take over.

The 'baptism of the Holy Spirit' is therefore a central aspect of black pentecostal spirituality in that it encourages the individual to seek for a personal spiritual experience or encounter with the divine, along with allowing them to feel a part of a wider spiritual community empowered to serve. There are however, times when the distinction between the 'filled' and the 'unfilled' gets too hierarchical, engendering a feeling of inadequacy among those who are not filled and a feeling of complacency among those who have been filled and speak in tongues. It is at such times that it is worth being reminded that speaking in tongues is just the

---

18 Rudolf Otto, *The Idea of the Holy* (OUP, 1950).

'initial evidence' and not the 'final' evidence of the baptism of the Holy Spirit. The demonstration of the fruits and the other gifts of the Holy Spirit are also valuable evidence that the Holy Spirit is active in the life of a believer and should be sought with equal enthusiasm and vigour.

One of the strengths of black pentecostalism is its emphasis on the power of the Holy Spirit for ministry and evangelism in the life of the believer. However, its one-dimensional emphasis on the role and function of the Holy Spirit, namely the speaking with tongues, can be rather unhealthy and very misleading. The idea that a person has not attained spiritual maturity—if indeed that can be attained—until they speak with tongues, has placed an unhelpful obsession with 'speaking with tongues' to the neglect of other aspects of the Spirit's work. It is also unfortunate that the Holy Spirit 'possession trance' is often nothing more than 'power play,' by many with their own agendas, which is a dangerous game.

It may be appropriate here for me to make a distinction between pentecostalism and the 'charismatic movement'—which also believes in speaking with tongues—which rose to prominence in the 1960s. Some charismatics consider themselves to be within the pentecostal tradition but do not consider speaking with tongues as *the* authenticating evidence of the 'baptism of the Holy Spirit.'

Holy Communion

Otherwise known as the Lord's supper or the Eucharist, holy communion is observed within the black pentecostal tradition. The frequency with which it is observed varies from church to church, though it usually takes place four to six times a year on average. This is, of course, in stark contrast to the Anglican and Catholic traditions where it is observed each week. Usually the service would begin with a few songs and choruses—which would be selectively or randomly chosen—reminiscent of the death of Christ and his journey to the cross. There would then follow a period of silent meditation and prayers of thanksgiving. The minister would then admonish the congregation to come to the Lord's table with a pure and holy heart. One of the emphases of this sacrament is the importance of being right with God and with each other. Some people may feel that they have not been living up to God's standard and therefore abstain from participating. The bread is often the traditional West Indian 'hard-dough bread' and the wine is non-alcoholic, usually grape juice. Some churches have a liturgical service book which sets out a format which the service could take, others read the passage from 1 Corinthians 11 and explain it as they serve the bread and wine to the servers. The wine is usually served in a small glass and each person waits till all have received before they partake. Although the question of consubstantiation or transubstantiation is not an issue within this context—which holds firmly to the symbolic representation understanding—there is a clear expectation and acknowledgement of the presence of Christ.

There is also a strong feeling of community participation in this sacrament which is reinforced by foot-washing. This is, for black pentecostal Christians, just as important as the bread and the wine. Through the bread and the wine we respond to God in the light of what he has done for us through Christ Jesus. Through the act of foot-washing we respond to each other as recipients of God's grace. The men and the women move into separate rooms, the basins and the towels are brought out and we wash each other's feet. The foot-washing among the men is very interesting to observe.

Apart from being one of the few times that the men of the church get together, it is a time when real fellowship amongst the men takes place. Although the leadership of the church is comprised predominantly of men, the overwhelming majority of the church population consists of women. It is often said—and it is probably true—that the women are the backbone of the church. They are far more active than the men, more outgoing and more involved. Perhaps because of the disparity in numbers, the lay men are usually alienated and reserved in comparison to the lay women. As the women leave to wash each other's feet—which usually mean more than two-thirds of the congregation have left—there is often a sudden feeling of vulnerability as the men seek to hold everything together. The harmonious female voices are no longer present to supplement the deeper male voices. The seating takes a long time to re-arrange and there is a strange anxiety in the air. In a culture where men often project a certain image which involves suppressing personal emotion or vulnerability, inner feelings—which I distinguish from 'spiritual emotionalism'—are often repressed beneath the triumphalism of pentecostalism. But the act of seeing, touching, washing and drying the feet of another brother in a worship setting somehow reminds us of the importance of seeing each other as people, with physical and emotional and not just spiritual needs. This seems to recapture something of the holistic spirituality which I think is a very important part of the holy communion.

Preaching of the Word

The black pentecostal preacher is the medium of divine revelation through whom the word of God is imparted to the people. He or she is the vessel through which the Almighty communicates to the congregation. Because God is the author of the word, it must be dynamic and filled with power. In the 1950s and 60s, a preacher would be highly respected if he or she could preach without notes. The subconscious and conscious thinking behind this was that God was then speaking directly through the preacher. What was being said, therefore, was not a product of human study or intellectualization, but the inspired word of God. Among the older generation there is still an element of this anti-intellectualism, in the sense that the preacher must be a passive vessel. The pulpit is the symbol of divine revelation, it is the place where God speaks through the preacher and therefore there is great emphasis placed on the holiness of the one who stands in it. It is often said by the older members that 'this is a dreadful place; few can stand here.' Those who ascend it for the first time do so knowing that they are standing in a 'dreadful' place and constantly ask for prayer.

Black pentecostal preaching is *dialogical*. There is an ongoing dialogue between the preacher and the people, the pulpit engaging in dynamic interaction with the pew, in a way which is reminiscent of the 'call and response' within African tradition.[19] The preacher will make a point during the course of his sermon (the call) and then expect a response from the congregation, usually 'Amen' or 'Praise the Lord.' It is not just a call for mere verbal response, as Joel Edwards rightly observes, but a challenge to the congregation to affirm the truth of the spoken word. It also allows the preacher to 'test the waters' to see if the congregation affirms what he or she is saying, the louder and more robust the 'Amen' and the 'Hallelujah' the more he or she knows the message is being received. The preacher sometimes leaves the pulpit and moves amongst the people whilst still preaching, shaking people's hands and calling out individuals' names. For example, the preacher may walk up to a member of the congregation, take them by the hand and passionately utter 'sister Johnson, sometimes you can't see a way out, but the Lord makes a way where there was no way...' This type of oral preaching style, when based firmly on sound biblical theology and personal devotion, is very powerful.

The use of the Bible is very significant in black pentecostal preaching. The infallibility and inerrancy of holy writ is the consensus on which the preacher and the congregation stand. Often the preacher will reinforce this by declaring out loud part of a passage of Scripture and the congregation will in one voice complete it. For example, the preacher will shout 'And God so loved the world...' and the congregation will cry out, '...that he gave his only begotten Son.' This again is a classic demonstration of the enactment of the call and response tradition mentioned above.

Although pentecostal preachers are known for their sound bites, clichés and fiery delivery, content is very important. A few years ago an American preacher came as the guest speaker for our national convention. At these conventions the success of the whole event often rests on the shoulders of the preacher—he or she better be 'on fire,' so to speak. This particular preacher, determined to make the auditorium erupt with praises, started shouting and stamping his feet right from the start, using mainly sound bites and key 'push button phrases' such as:

'We need to get back to the old time religion, when the church was the church and the world was the world and you could tell the difference.'
or
'I'm so glad that my soul has been washed in the blood of the lamb.'

Under normal circumstances these catch phrases are used to supplement a message causing the congregation to respond enthusiastically. However, on this occasion, the response was nothing more than a few isolated 'Amen's and 'Praise the Lord's. What he failed to realize—as many from the historical churches do—is

---

19 On preaching see Martin Simmonds, *A Portrayal of Identity: A study of the Life of Worship of the First United Church of Jesus Christ (Apostolic) UK* (Unpublished M Phil dissertation: University of Birmingham, May 1988) and Joel Edwards (ed), *Let's Praise Him Again: An African-Caribbean Perspective on Worship* (Kingsway, 1992), especially pages 53–58.

that the shouting and praising experienced in a black pentecostal setting as a response to the preached word is usually a reply to biblical principals and truths contextually translated and dramatized in such a way that it resonates with the experience and the lives of the listeners. Joel Edwards comments that 'A rambling preacher without content or context is no more helpful to a congregation than the desperate scream of a drowning man, and the two things are not entirely dissimilar.'[20]

There were times when theological training was not given such a high priority, being viewed as nothing more than 'man-made knowledge,' which bears the hallmarks of the anti-intellectualism of the Holiness movement. However, the black pentecostal audience in Britain has to a large extent changed, with an increasingly younger membership demanding more than the nostalgic anecdote of life on the farm back home in the West Indies and the theological language culturally inaccessible to the British-born black members. The compulsion that ministers are to undergo theological training before entering the ministry has also raised the theological expectation of the congregation.

Black pentecostal preaching in America, Caribbean and in the UK is largely extemporary, taking a particular subject or theme, with a series of texts—quoted verbally or read—and developing a number of points on the way to the grand crescendo at the end. Narrative and orality are, therefore, key elements within the black pentecostal preaching tradition.

Water Baptism

The baptism service of a black pentecostal church often takes place at a swimming pool, though a number black pentecostal churches now have their own baptismal. The use of the swimming pool is reminiscent of the riverside baptism service, back in the West Indies. Some churches make special trips to the coast for this occasion.[21]

The candidates are dressed in white apparel, to signify their purity and sanctification and are asked to give a testimony to those who have come to witness the public demonstration of their commitment to Christ. Although the black pentecostal churches are notorious for their (poor) time-keeping, there are a few occasions when you can guarantee that the members and visitors will be early, and a baptism service is one of those times. In preparation for baptism, the candidates are encouraged to invite their entire family, along with their work, college or school friends. During the service there is a strong emphasis on separation from 'worldliness' which is normally used to mean going to the pub, discos, night clubs, wearing certain items of clothing, jewellery, swearing, smoking and drinking alcohol. Fortunately, the whole notion of 'worldliness' and the meaning of being separate from the world have today acquired a deeper and less superficial

20 Joel Edwards, *op cit*, p 58.
21 *Black Christians: Black Church Traditions in Britain*, (A resource pack jointly produced by the Centre for Black and White Christian Partnership and Westhill RE Centre, Selly Oak Colleges, Birmingham, 1995).

emphasis. This represents a new wave of thinking within black pentecostal ecclesiology, driven by the second generation of British-born Christians as well as the theological enlightenment now in full swing across many of these churches. But for some, 'worldliness' still carries the meaning of refraining from the above mentioned activities in true Holiness tradition. The baptism of the candidates is by full immersion in the name of the Father, the Son and the Holy Spirit, according to the Trinitarian tradition, as opposed to in 'Jesus' name,' which is the Apostolic or 'Jesus only' tradition. The candidate emerges from the watery grave to the burst of lively choruses which graphically illustrate the new life that the individual has come into. Two such choruses which are sung are:

> Goodbye world, I'll stay no longer with you,
> Goodbye pleasures of sin, I'll stay no longer with you,
> I've made up my mind to go God's way the rest of my life,
> I've made up my mind to go God's way the rest of my life,

or

> I'm a new creation, I'm a brand new man,
> Old things have passed away, I'm born again.
> More than a conqueror, that's who I am,
> I'm a new creation, I'm a brand new man.

After the baptism of the candidates, the minister usually makes an appeal to the unconverted—who would have heard a sermon preceding the baptism—to make a public response. The text often referred to is Acts 8.26-40, in which Philip baptized the Ethiopian eunuch immediately after he heard and received the gospel. The minister therefore boldly proclaims 'Here is water, what doth hinder you?' Baptism as a sacrament within black pentecostal tradition is a re-enactment of the death and resurrection of Christ. It is the outward demonstration of the inward work of grace. It signifies the death of the former life and a resurrection to a new life in Christ Jesus. Through water baptism, the believer identifies with Christ's death and resurrection. The community involvement in the baptism service is also very significant. The candidates are not just baptized into the mystical body of Christ, but also into the faith community. This is indicative of the fact that religion within this context is not a private affair but the business of the whole community who share in this corporate faith of which the individual is a part. This is one of the reasons why public testimonies are a regular feature of black pentecostal worship.

Worshipping Community

In African traditionalism song was an expression of the community's view of the world and its place in it. These songs were to black people what history books were to white people. Through song, story and history, initiation of the young into adulthood, death, marriage and belief were recorded. It was this African background that made it impossible for slaves to accept a religion that denigrated

16

their 'personhood.' Instead they combined the religion of the ancestor with the Christian gospel and created a spirituality of song that participated in their liberation from earthly bondage. It is this notion of and appreciation for the genre of song that is at the core of black pentecostal worship.

Many white Christians consider the worship of black pentecostal churches quite eccentric and excessive and can only cope with it in short doses. However, the degree of excessiveness and eccentricity must be measured against the degree of thankfulness that we feel is due to God for keeping us as a people through a history of oppression and slavery. It seems that Simon the Pharisee found this type of appreciation to be excessive and improper too, in Luke 7.41-43:

> 'There was a certain creditor who had two debtors. One owed five hundred denarii, and the other fifty. And when they had nothing with which to repay, he freely forgave them both. Tell Me, therefore, which one of them will love him more?' Simon answered and said 'I suppose the one whom he forgave more.' Jesus answered and said 'You have rightly judged.'

It is this tenet that governs the manner of worship in the black pentecostal church.[22]

Black pentecostalism has inherited much of its 'song culture' from the negro spirituals. Many of the songs from the nineteenth-century 'Holiness' movement are preserved within traditional hymnals and have become part and parcel of our history. They are often sung by the senior members of the church who form duets and quartets, sounding out each part—bass, treble and soprano with a heavenly melody. Three examples are:

> Some glad morning when this life is o'er
> I'll fly away,
> To a home on God's celestial shore,
> I'll fly away.

or

> Swing low sweet chariot
> coming forth to carry me home,
> Swing low sweet chariot,
> coming forth to carry me home

and

> We'll soon be done, with trouble and trials,
> In that home, on the other side
> I'm going to shake my hand with the elder;
> Tell all the people good morning,
> Sit down beside my Jesus,
> Sit down and rest a little while.

---

22 Tony Evans, *Let's Get to Know Each Other: What White Christians Should Know about Black Christians* (Thomas Nelson Publishers, 1995) p 97.

Traditional hymns sung within the black pentecostal tradition are often improvised and changed as they are reinterpreted within the milieu of the black worship community. For example, 'Amazing Grace' sounds distinctively different when you hear it in a black pentecostal church setting, compared to the way you hear it sung in a white church setting. I doubt seriously if the slave trader John Newton would have envisioned the black pentecostal version of his well known hymn with its definitive cadence.

More recently these historical sounds are giving way to the more contemporary feel which is strongly influenced by the contemporary gospel music scene from across the Atlantic. Joel Edwards remarks:

> 'This change is coming about largely through the music of younger Christians. The traditional hymns of Sankey and Moody and the Redemption Hymnal are quietly giving way to the American choir sound. Even the more recent country western style of the Chuck Wagon Gang and popular denominational hymnals loved by many senior adults is gently being set aside for the more contemporary sounds of black American songs or the worship chorus culture of British Christian songwriters like Graham Kendrick.'[23]

This transition in the gospel music culture currently taking place is a very significant one and marks a turning point in the history of black pentecostal spirituality in Britain. Second and third generation black Christians, caught between cultures, are now making their mark on the 'church music' tradition and spirituality generally, authenticating their own interpretation, creating their own genre of song. A case in point has been the emergence of black pentecostal choirs of the eighties and nineties which have given black British gospel music national and international acclaim. More recently, the sounds of 'rap music' and 'Ragga' which belong to black secular contemporary music culture, otherwise known as 'street music,' are now given Christian lyrics and are used by younger black Christians as a witness to their contemporaries, for whom even the more recent choir music— not to mention Moody and Sankey—is of a different age. Beneath this renaissance of song is a quest for an authentic spirituality which is born out of the context of black British Christian youth culture, a spirituality that is at the heart of their struggles, frustrations and identity, one which is not simply imported from African or the Caribbean, but which is able to be transformed by the British context in order for it to remain relevant.

Fasting and Prayer

Weekly fasting and prayer services are part of a regular diet for black pentecostal Christians. Black pentecostals believe in the power of prayer. In the early days of the Holiness movement, believers who were critically ill often refused to see a doctor, believing that this would be to put one's faith in humans rather than God.

---

23 Joel Edwards (ed), *op cit*, p 72.

Although this is not the case today, there is still a strong belief in the healing power of God 'through the blood of Jesus Christ.' Individual and private prayers have very little room in this context; prayer is a corporate affair.

About a year after I became a Christian I remember attending a youth service within an Anglican church. We were told to break up into groups and pray about a particular issue. The leader of our group began praying. I then took this as the signal for all of us to start praying, so I immediately started praying at the same time as the leader of the group. To my surprise the group leader stopped praying and waited till I finished; furthermore, I was the only one praying. Corporate prayer, I soon discovered, had here a different meaning fom the one I had been accustomed to. To pray in a black pentecostal setting is more than to have a quiet conversation with God, as one would speak to a friend. Prayer is the invocation of the Almighty. In prayer, believers call down the power of God to act or to intercede on their behalf. It is quite common for the church to engage in prayer all night long, in what is sometimes known as a 'tarrying service.' The black pentecostal believer prays till he or she 'breaks through,' which means there is a overwhelming sense of the presence of God as the power of the Holy Spirit fills the church, leaving believers ecstatic and totally intoxicated with the Holy Spirit. Quite often prayers are supplemented with fasting. Although fasting may take place at a fixed period—once or twice a month—usually it takes place during a crisis or when the community is confronted with a desperate need. Believers are known to do without food for days when seeking God regarding a particular problem.

4
Black Pentecostal Spirituality and Black Culture

The tension between the gospel and culture is a daily reality in the black pentecostal church. Richard Niebuhr highlights the difficulty that is inherent in the whole process of defining what is 'gospel' and what is 'culture' and urges caution when trying to discern between them.[24] There are areas of both conflict and consensus between the spirituality of black pentecostalism and African and Caribbean culture.

Funerals

A few months ago I conducted a funeral service at my local church. Funerals are usually well attended and so well-wishers often come early, ensuring that they secure a seat for a service that could last anything up to two hours. Whilst waiting for the funeral party to arrive, I overheard a conversation between two elderly people, a man and a woman. 'Aoo dead' (who's dead) the old man asked, 'Mas Gee, from duna St Tann's' (Mr Gee from down St Ann's).[25] Attending a funeral without knowing who has actually died is very common within the black community. Death is not and cannot be a private or family affair; it involves the entire community. This notion of the priority of the community over and above the individual is echoed by the now familiar phrase of John Mbiti, an Africa theologian: 'I am because we are, because we are I am.'[26] According to African traditional religion to die is not to cease to be, but to be elevated to the realm of the spirits or ancestors. According to African philosophy the community does not only consist of the living, but of the dead also.

After the death of a loved one, the bereaved person is all too aware that they will have to start preparing the traditional Caribbean cuisine: chicken and rice, fried fish and curried mutton with rice for the throng of people—many of whom they will have never set eyes on before—for the start of what is called 'nine nights.' This is the nine-day period in which the community gathers at the house of the deceased to mourn with and to comfort the bereaved family. During these nine nights people stay up till the early hours of the morning telling stories of the times they had with the person who has now passed away. Others play dominoes and listen to music.

In 1992 whilst studying at St John's College, Nottingham, I was fortunate to be able to spend a summer term in Kenya. Whilst there, among the Turkana people of northern Kenya, that I was able—to my surprise—to witness first-hand the African origin of these funeral rituals whilst attending the funeral of a local farmer.

---

24 Richard Niebuhr, *Christ and Culture* (New York: Harper & Row, 1975) p 30.
25 This is the traditional West Indian dialect otherwise known as 'Patois.'
26 John Mbiti, *African Religions and Philosophy* (London: SPCK, 1969) p 49.

I recognized that there were no professional gravediggers, but the privilege of burial was reserved for the family and relatives. This shed light on our insistence—to the grave diggers' delight—on burying our own dead. At a black funeral, smartly dressed friends, relatives and community members take it in turn to fill in the grave, whilst songs like 'Sleep on beloved, sleep and take your rest/ We love you dear, but Jesus loves you best/Good night, good night, good night,' ring out in the background. The idea that a funeral service and burial can be 'contracted out' to 'professionals'—which would ostensibly mean the secularizing of the whole process—is repugnant to black people.

Time

There is a familiar saying in Africa and the Caribbean which says, 'You Europeans have watches but we Africans have time.' Black pentecostals are notorious for their time-keeping. The reasons for this are complex and historical. Within a black pentecostal church, it is not unusual for a seven o'clock service to finally get underway thirty minutes later, during which time members come trickling in and the necessary arrangements and changes are made to the furniture. If one is inviting a black person to a service, one can feel confident that they will know a seven o'clock start means, well, thereabouts. However, when inviting a white person, particularly from one of the historical churches, telling them seven o'clock start usually means they will show up at a quarter to seven, which could be embarrassing if they are the first to arrive. Therefore, telling them seven thirty may be more appropriate.

When two black people are deciding on the specific time to meet, they often joke about whether the time will be BMT (black man's time) or GMT (Greenwich mean time). This flexibility with time also extends to the time at which the service ends. It is not unusual for a service which is scheduled to end at nine o'clock to go on till eleven or even twelve o'clock at night. This is often the case during revival services or on occasions when, as we say, 'the Spirit takes over.'

Our notion of time goes back to the Caribbean and ultimately African traditionalism. In Africa, for example, time is not linear, characterized by the passing of seconds, minutes and hours, as it is in a European context, but it is the encounter with specific events that occur during the passing of the day. This understanding explains why the idea of time in our traditional context is more characterized by morning, noon and night than by the twenty-four-hour clock. On my first visit to Jamaica, some fifteen years ago, I remember being taken somewhat by surprise by the contrast between their pace of life and the one I had become accustomed to. There it was infinitely slower, which was not just because of the warm climate, but because of their whole outlook on the world. It took my uncle and I two whole hours to walk a hundred yards, due to him stopping and talking at every corner, engaging in the deep conversation that happens daily. It is a culture in which people encounter people on a deeper and much more personal and meaningful level. One hot afternoon on the veranda of my sister's house in Montego Bay, during the same visit, I watched as my uncle and his friend sat down and

21

talked unremittingly for six and a half hours, joking and laughing throughout. I thought to myself, what do they have to talk about so intensively when they see each other almost every other day? On reflection, the times spent with God and each other are the essence and building blocks of a true spirituality of community. Beneath the black pentecostal's rebellion to conform to a 'diary culture' in which 'time is money'—the corollary of which is, 'distribute with extreme caution'—is the recognition that one should not be too enslaved by the constraint, of something which is a product of human culture. It is at such time that it is apt to acknowledge that 'the Sabbath was made for people and not people for the Sabbath.'

Dreams

A dream is defined by the *Concise Oxford Dictionary* as a 'series of pictures or event in the mind of the sleeping person.' This definition of dreams bears the hallmarks of cultural limitations, describing dreams from a Western perspective. One of the main differences between a western European understanding and the black pentecostal understanding of dreams is that, for the West, the starting point is almost always the unconscious mind, whereas for the black pentecostal the starting point is belief in a spiritual world. For Freud, the only architect of dreams was the unconscious mind. For us, the architect of dreams is a transcendent God. Dreams then, from a black pentecostal perspective, are essentially about communication, communication with a transcendent spiritual community which forms part of the wider community. Senghor of Sengal has spoken of a 'tender bridge' between the living and the dead in which dreams are the 'arches of the bridge.' Another contrast between a Western and a black pentecostal understanding is that the black pentecostal is not interested in the dream *per se*, but the message that has been communicated through the dream which is not for individual psychoanalysis, but a sign for the whole community. This is more than a recognition that dreams have meaning, it is that the world of dreams is a living reality in which spirits communicate with the dreamer. Dreams therefore, are not an end in themselves but a means to an end, the end being the message conveyed through the dream which will have real consequences.

Within a black pentecostal context dreams are functional. Some are 'warning dreams,' warning an individual or the community of what will happen if a certain course of action takes place; others are 'predictive dreams' which are largely predictions of every day occurrences. Often they are about practical things such as a sudden visit by a friend or relative, as well as more serious issues such as death, births, sickness and healing. It is not uncommon to hear one of the mothers of the church say 'Sumwan agoo dead' (someone is going to die). 'Me dream see it laas night' (I saw it in a dream last night). Due to their proven track record, we know these may not be idle speculations but prophetic utterances. 'Nightmare dreams' are usually associated with being attacked by evil spirits. Dream interpretation is also important. Within this context, dreams can be understood if the dream image (also called dream motif) is properly interpreted. Usually there is someone who is unofficially acknowledged as being able to interpret dreams to whom members of the congregation go for interpretation of dreams which may be of concern to them. This tradition, however, is slowly dying out. It is interesting to note that in dream interpretation they are not doing psychoanalysis but semiotics, pointing the dreamer, and/or the community, to the true meaning of the dream: warning, nightmare, prediction or of no significance at all.[27]

Dreams, then, occupy a unique function within black pentecostalism, involving the way we understand ourselves in the context of our community and the world which we inhabit, and the way we relate to and place meaning on transcendent spiritual realities and the events of everyday life. To deny the spiritual reality of dreams is to shut out a part of our spiritual capacity which is a large part of who we are. This is an area of spirituality often neglected in other Western Christian traditions.[28]

Taboo and Superstition

The spirituality of black pentecostalism is interspersed with superstitions and taboos which have filtered through from West Africa and the Caribbean oral tradition. Many of these taboos and superstition are so integral to Caribbean culture that they have become cultural norms. These cultural norms are still observed—particularly by the first generation black immigrant Christians—in spite of their inherent contradictions to Christian theology and their detachment from their original context.

During my visit to Jamaica referred to earlier I was intrigued when my sister, who had spent all her life in Jamaica, pointed out to me that the bird perched on the roof of the veranda, which I had observed for a number of days, was in fact 'granny.' Granny had died two years ago. I decided to give her the benefit of my western rational education. I proceeded to explain the biblical teaching on death. I could tell by the way she responded that she was not used to this cultural norm being challenged, though she had spent most of her life in a Christian context. Further, she did not seem to have a problem with holding these two conflicting ideas at the same time—the biblical view that after death people cannot come back and join their family and friends, and the belief common within African-Caribbean tradition that they can and they do, with the specific purpose of watching over and protecting the community from evil forces.

Today, with the proliferation of pentecostal theological colleges and Bible schools, along with the assimilation of black British-born Christians into the church ranks, traditional beliefs are often latent, occasionally surfacing in certain life-changing events such as death, birth and marriage. During my home visits to bereaved families I am often fascinated by some of these religiously observed taboos and superstitions passed down through Caribbean oral culture. They include, for example, the wearing of red or black underwear by the spouse of a

---

27 See further Russ Parker's *Dreams and Spirituality* (Grove Spirituality booklet S 15).
28 See author's unpublished dissertation, *An African Contribution to a Christian Theology of Dreams in a Western Context* (University of Derby, 1995).

deceased husband or wife at nights until the day of the funeral. This is to prevent the spirit of the dead person coming back to have sexual intercourse with his or her spouse. If during a wedding the wedding cake falls to the ground, this is a bad omen, and would mean that either bride or groom will shortly pass away or that the marriage will not last long. It is also said that nine days after the birth of a baby, a woman is not to go out doors, to prevent a bad omen. Mystical powers are attributed to Christian symbols such as the Bible and olive oil. It is said if you open the Bible of a black pentecostal Christian you will automatically end up at the 23rd Psalm. The Bible is kept open at this place all the time and is often laid on the bed in a black Christian home to keep away evil spirits. Anointing someone with olive oil is also said to do this. This strange combination of superstition, fables, taboos, and 'duppy' (ghost) stories, passed on through West Indian oral tradition, gives the spirituality of black pentecostalism its distinctive character.

5
Conclusion

In this brief exploration of black pentecostal spirituality, I have sought to demonstrate that spirituality and community are not necessarily separate realities, but are rather inextricably linked. What the black pentecostal spirituality teaches us is that we do not find out who we are in the flight of the alone to the Alone, escaping from turmoil into tranquillity, but only in the community or ordinary life in which we need others to help us to understand our own significance. The word used for this in the New Testament is *koinonia*. Together with a more vital understanding of God this experience of being part of a living fellowship, a greater whole, given meaning and identity by our solidarity in Christ, is something the black pentecostal tradition can teach other churches.

I believe that the question of where, how and among whom modern pentecostalism came to birth is very significant. Like the story of the ancient Israelites and the life of Jesus of Nazareth, it is another example of God using people from the underside of life to accomplish his divine purpose. God's pouring of the new blessing on William Joseph Seymour, a one-eyed black preacher, and a group of social outcasts in 1906 in Azusa Street, Los Angeles, USA is what has shaped our spirituality to make it what it is today.

The great temptation facing black pentecostals today is to forget or minimize the circumstances of our birth, to try to blend into the religious and social atmosphere around us. If we deny our origin we also deprive ourselves of a future. Yet we most not be enslaved by our past but allow God through the power of the Holy Spirit to continue renewing us. This, after all, is the reason why we sing.